Designing the Future: Architectural Trends in New Chinese Cities

Table of Contents

Designing the Future: Architectural Trends in New Chinese Cities

By Roberto Miguel Rodriguez

Chapter 1: Introduction

Background and context of Chinese urban development

China's rapid urbanization in recent years has been nothing short of extraordinary. As the country strives for economic growth and development, its cities have become hubs of innovation, opportunity, and cultural exchange. However, this urbanization has also brought about numerous challenges, such as environmental degradation, social inequality, and the loss of cultural heritage.

Sustainable urban planning in Chinese cities has emerged as a critical approach to address these challenges. With a focus on minimizing environmental impact and promoting social equity, sustainable urban planning aims to create livable and resilient cities for current and future generations. This approach involves integrating green spaces, promoting energy-efficient buildings, and implementing sustainable transportation systems.

Cultural preservation and heritage conservation in new Chinese cities is another aspect that urban planners are increasingly focusing on. China's rich history and diverse cultural heritage are at risk of being overshadowed by modern development. Therefore, efforts are being made to protect and restore historic buildings, traditional neighborhoods, and cultural landmarks. These preservation initiatives not only contribute to the preservation of cultural identity but also attract tourists and promote economic development.

Smart city technologies and innovations in Chinese urban development have also gained momentum in recent years. With the aim of enhancing efficiency, connectivity, and sustainability, cities across China are adopting cutting-edge technologies such as Internet of Things (IoT), artificial intelligence (AI), and big data analytics. These technologies enable improved resource management, optimized transportation systems, and enhanced public services.

Urban transportation systems and infrastructure play a crucial role in the development of Chinese cities. As urban populations grow, the demand for efficient and sustainable transportation options intensifies. Chinese cities are investing heavily in public transportation systems, including metro networks, high-speed rail, and bike-sharing programs. These initiatives not only reduce traffic congestion and air pollution but also improve accessibility and mobility for all residents.

Vertical farming and urban agriculture are emerging trends in Chinese urban planning. With limited arable land and a growing population, urban agriculture offers a solution to food security and self-sufficiency. Vertical farms, rooftop gardens, and community gardens are being integrated into urban designs, providing fresh produce and promoting sustainable food production practices.

Eco-friendly and green building practices are gaining prominence in new Chinese cities. With a focus on energy efficiency, water conservation, and waste management, green buildings contribute to reducing the carbon footprint and promoting a healthier living environment. Sustainable building materials, passive design strategies, and renewable energy sources are being incorporated into urban development projects.

Social and community development are key considerations for urban planners in Chinese cities. As urbanization progresses, social cohesion and community well-being become increasingly important. Efforts are being made to create inclusive and accessible public spaces, promote social integration, and provide affordable housing options for all residents.

Urban resilience and disaster management have become critical aspects of Chinese urban development. As cities face the challenges of climate change and natural disasters, resilience strategies are being implemented to enhance preparedness, response, and recovery. These strategies include flood control measures, urban greening initiatives, and the integration of disaster risk reduction into urban planning.

Urban poverty alleviation and inclusive growth strategies are vital for addressing social inequalities in Chinese cities. Despite the economic progress, urban poverty remains a significant concern. The government, along with various stakeholders, is implementing poverty alleviation programs, providing access to education, healthcare, and employment opportunities, and promoting inclusive growth strategies to ensure that no one is left behind.

Urban design and architectural trends in new Chinese cities are constantly evolving. From iconic skyline developments to mixed-use neighborhoods and sustainable urban designs, Chinese cities are redefining the urban landscape. Innovative architectural concepts, such as green roofs, pedestrian-friendly streetscapes, and adaptive reuse of historic buildings, are transforming the urban fabric and creating unique cityscapes.

In conclusion, Chinese urban development is a complex and dynamic process that requires careful consideration of various factors. Sustainable urban planning, cultural preservation, smart city technologies, transportation systems, vertical farming, eco-friendly building practices, social development, resilience, poverty alleviation, and urban design trends are all crucial elements in shaping the future of Chinese cities. By addressing these aspects, urban planners can create cities that are not only economically prosperous but also socially inclusive, environmentally sustainable, and culturally vibrant.

Purpose and significance of the book

Designing the Future: Architectural Trends in New Chinese Cities is a comprehensive exploration of the various aspects of urban planning and development in China. This subchapter aims to highlight the purpose and significance of the book in addressing the specific needs and interests of urban planners, as well as the various niches within the field of sustainable urban planning, cultural preservation, smart city technologies, urban transportation systems, vertical farming, eco-friendly building practices, social and community development, urban resilience, poverty alleviation, and urban design and architectural trends in new Chinese cities.

For urban planners, this book serves as a valuable resource providing insights into the latest architectural trends and urban planning strategies in Chinese cities. It offers a comprehensive analysis of the challenges and opportunities faced by urban planners in creating sustainable, livable, and resilient cities. Through case studies and expert interviews, urban planners can gain a deeper understanding of the unique complexities and dynamics of Chinese urban development.

Furthermore, this book caters to the specific niches within the field of urban planning in China. For those interested in sustainable urban planning, it delves into the various strategies and initiatives undertaken in Chinese cities to promote environmental consciousness and resource efficiency. The chapter on cultural preservation and heritage conservation examines the efforts made to safeguard China's rich cultural heritage amidst rapid urbanization. The section on smart city technologies and innovations explores the role of technology in enhancing urban efficiency and quality of life. Similarly, other niches such as urban transportation systems, vertical farming, eco-friendly building practices, social and community development, urban resilience, poverty alleviation, and inclusive growth strategies are all addressed within the book.

By addressing these specific niches, the book provides a holistic understanding of the multidimensional nature of urban planning in China. It promotes interdisciplinary collaboration and encourages urban planners to adopt innovative approaches that integrate various aspects of urban development.

In conclusion, Designing the Future: Architectural Trends in New Chinese Cities serves as a comprehensive guide for urban planners, offering valuable insights into the challenges, opportunities, and best practices in sustainable urban planning, cultural preservation, smart city technologies, urban transportation systems, vertical farming, eco-friendly building practices, social and community development, urban resilience, poverty alleviation, and urban design and architectural trends in new Chinese cities. It is an essential resource for any urban planner seeking to navigate the complexities of urban development in China and contribute to the creation of vibrant, resilient, and sustainable cities.

Chapter 2: Sustainable Urban Planning in Chinese Cities

Principles of sustainable urban planning

Urban planning plays a crucial role in shaping the development of cities, and in the context of rapidly growing Chinese cities, it becomes even more important to focus on sustainable practices. The principles of sustainable urban planning provide a framework for creating livable, resilient, and environmentally friendly cities that can meet the needs of present and future generations. This subchapter explores key principles that urban planners should consider when designing and developing new Chinese cities.

Firstly, sustainable urban planning should prioritize the protection and preservation of cultural heritage. As Chinese cities undergo rapid modernization, it is essential to safeguard the rich cultural heritage that exists within these urban areas. By incorporating traditional architectural styles, historical landmarks, and cultural practices into urban design, planners can create a sense of place and identity, while also promoting tourism and economic growth.

Another principle is the integration of smart city technologies and innovations. Chinese cities are at the forefront of utilizing technology to enhance urban development. By incorporating smart infrastructure, data-driven decision-making, and efficient resource management systems, cities can optimize energy consumption, reduce waste, and improve the quality of life for residents.

Urban transportation systems and infrastructure also play a vital role in sustainable urban planning. Chinese cities face significant challenges in managing traffic congestion and reducing pollution. Planners should prioritize the development of affordable and efficient public transportation systems, such as metro networks and bus rapid transit, to encourage sustainable modes of commuting and reduce reliance on private vehicles.

Incorporating vertical farming and urban agriculture into urban planning can address food security and promote sustainable practices. By utilizing vertical space, cities can produce fresh produce locally, reducing the carbon footprint associated with long-distance transportation of food and enhancing the resilience of the urban food system.

Eco-friendly and green building practices are essential for sustainable urban planning. Incorporating energy-efficient design, renewable energy sources, and green spaces into building projects can reduce carbon emissions, improve air quality, and enhance the well-being of urban residents.

Social and community development should be at the core of sustainable urban planning. By creating inclusive and vibrant neighborhoods, cities can foster a sense of community, promote social integration, and improve the quality of life for all residents.

Lastly, urban resilience and disaster management strategies are crucial in the face of increasingly frequent natural disasters. By integrating climate adaptation measures, such as flood-resistant infrastructure and green spaces, cities can enhance their ability to withstand and recover from shocks and stresses.

In conclusion, sustainable urban planning in Chinese cities should adhere to principles that prioritize cultural preservation, smart city technologies, efficient transportation systems, vertical farming, eco-friendly building practices, social development, resilience, and inclusive growth strategies. By embracing these principles, urban planners can create vibrant, livable, and environmentally conscious cities that meet the needs of present and future generations.

Implementation of sustainable practices in Chinese cities

China's rapid urbanization has presented both challenges and opportunities in terms of sustainability. As urban planners, it is crucial to address these issues and implement sustainable practices in Chinese cities to ensure long-term environmental, social, and economic well-being. This subchapter explores various strategies and initiatives that can be undertaken to achieve this goal.

One of the key aspects of sustainable urban planning in Chinese cities is cultural preservation and heritage conservation. As new cities are being built, it is important to preserve the rich cultural heritage and historical sites. This can be achieved through careful planning, adaptive reuse of existing structures, and the integration of traditional architectural elements into new developments.

In addition, the adoption of smart city technologies and innovations can greatly contribute to sustainable urban development. Smart transportation systems, energy-efficient buildings, and the use of renewable energy sources can help reduce carbon emissions and improve the overall quality of life for residents.

Urban transportation systems and infrastructure play a vital role in sustainable city planning. The development of efficient public transportation systems, pedestrian-friendly streets, and dedicated cycling lanes can help reduce congestion, promote active transportation, and improve air quality.

Vertical farming and urban agriculture are also gaining momentum in Chinese urban planning. By utilizing vertical spaces and implementing innovative farming techniques, cities can achieve food self-sufficiency, reduce transport distances, and minimize the environmental impact of agriculture.

Eco-friendly and green building practices should be integrated into new city developments. This includes the use of sustainable materials, energy-efficient design, and the incorporation of green spaces and vegetation into buildings.

Social and community development should be a priority in Chinese urban areas. Creating inclusive and vibrant neighborhoods, promoting social cohesion, and providing access to basic services and amenities are essential for the well-being of residents.

Urban resilience and disaster management strategies are crucial in Chinese cities, considering the increasing frequency of natural disasters. This involves developing robust infrastructure, implementing early warning systems, and establishing emergency response plans.

Furthermore, urban poverty alleviation and inclusive growth strategies are essential in addressing social inequality and promoting sustainable development. This can be achieved through targeted poverty reduction programs, affordable housing initiatives, and skill development programs for marginalized communities.

Lastly, urban design and architectural trends should embrace sustainability principles. This includes designing buildings and public spaces that promote energy efficiency, natural ventilation, and the use of renewable energy sources.

In conclusion, the implementation of sustainable practices in Chinese cities requires a holistic and integrated approach. By addressing key areas such as sustainable urban planning, cultural preservation, smart city technologies, transportation systems, vertical farming, eco-friendly building practices, social development, resilience, poverty alleviation, and architectural trends, urban planners can contribute to the creation of sustainable and livable cities in China.

Challenges and opportunities for sustainable urban planning in China

China's rapid urbanization has presented both challenges and opportunities for sustainable urban planning in the country. As urban planners grapple with the task of designing new cities and revitalizing existing ones, they face numerous obstacles to creating sustainable and livable urban environments. However, these challenges also open up avenues for innovation and creative solutions.

One of the primary challenges is the sheer scale of urbanization in China. With a population of over 1.4 billion people, the demand for urban spaces is immense. This puts pressure on planners to find ways to accommodate the growing population while minimizing the environmental impact. Additionally, the need to balance economic development with social and environmental sustainability presents a complex challenge.

Another key challenge is preserving China's rich cultural heritage and history while embracing modernization. Many new Chinese cities are built from scratch, often replacing traditional structures and neighborhoods. Urban planners must find ways to integrate cultural preservation and heritage conservation into their designs, ensuring that the new cities retain a sense of identity and authenticity.

However, these challenges also present opportunities for sustainable urban planning in China. The country's commitment to smart city technologies and innovations has the potential to transform urban development. By leveraging the power of data and technology, planners can create more efficient and environmentally friendly cities. From intelligent transportation systems to energy-efficient buildings, these innovations can improve the quality of life for urban residents while reducing resource consumption.

Furthermore, China's focus on vertical farming and urban agriculture offers a unique opportunity for sustainable food production in urban areas. By utilizing vertical spaces and innovative farming techniques, cities can become more self-sufficient in food production, reducing reliance on long-distance transportation and minimizing the carbon footprint associated with food consumption.

Eco-friendly and green building practices also play a crucial role in sustainable urban planning. China has made significant strides in promoting energy-efficient buildings and sustainable construction materials. By integrating green building practices into urban design, planners can create healthier and more environmentally friendly living spaces.

Social and community development is another important aspect of sustainable urban planning in China. As cities grow, it is essential to foster a sense of community and social cohesion. Planners can prioritize the development of public spaces, parks, and community centers, creating opportunities for social interaction and enhancing the overall quality of life.

In conclusion, the challenges and opportunities for sustainable urban planning in China are vast. From balancing economic development with environmental sustainability to preserving cultural heritage, urban planners have a complex task ahead. However, by embracing smart city technologies, promoting vertical farming and urban agriculture, adopting eco-friendly building practices, and prioritizing social and community development, planners can create sustainable and livable cities for future generations.

Chapter 3: Cultural Preservation and Heritage Conservation in New Chinese Cities

Importance of cultural preservation in urban development

In the rapidly evolving landscape of urban development in China, the importance of cultural preservation cannot be overstated. As urban planners, it is crucial to recognize the value of cultural heritage and incorporate it into our designs, creating sustainable and livable cities that celebrate the past while embracing the future.

Sustainable urban planning in Chinese cities is not just about creating environmentally friendly communities, but also about preserving the cultural identity of a place. By integrating cultural preservation into our designs, we can ensure that the unique heritage and traditions of a city are respected and maintained.

Cultural preservation and heritage conservation in new Chinese cities are essential for several reasons. Firstly, cultural heritage provides a sense of identity and belonging for residents. It connects them to their roots and creates a sense of pride in their community. By preserving cultural sites, buildings, and traditions, we can foster a strong sense of place and community in new Chinese cities.

Secondly, cultural preservation attracts tourism and boosts the economy. Many tourists are drawn to cities with a rich cultural heritage, as they offer a unique and authentic experience. By preserving and showcasing cultural sites, we can create sustainable tourism opportunities and stimulate economic growth.

Smart city technologies and innovations in Chinese urban development can be seamlessly integrated with cultural preservation efforts. For example, digital platforms can provide interactive experiences that educate residents and tourists about the history and significance of cultural sites. Augmented reality and virtual reality technologies can also be used to bring historical landmarks back to life, allowing people to experience the past in a modern and engaging way.

Furthermore, cultural preservation can be a catalyst for social and community development in Chinese urban areas. By involving local communities in the preservation process, we can empower them and create a sense of ownership and pride. This can lead to increased social cohesion, improved quality of life, and stronger community bonds.

In conclusion, cultural preservation plays a crucial role in sustainable urban planning in Chinese cities. By recognizing and embracing the cultural heritage of a place, we can create vibrant, livable, and economically prosperous cities that celebrate the past while building for the future. As urban planners, it is our responsibility to ensure that cultural preservation remains at the forefront of our designs, benefiting both current and future generations.

Strategies for heritage conservation in Chinese cities

As urban planners in the context of sustainable urban planning in Chinese cities, it is crucial to recognize the importance of cultural preservation and heritage conservation in new Chinese cities. Rapid urbanization and modernization have often resulted in the destruction of historical sites and the loss of cultural identity. Therefore, it is essential to implement effective strategies to safeguard and promote the rich heritage of Chinese cities. This subchapter will explore various strategies for heritage conservation in Chinese cities, focusing on sustainable approaches and innovative technologies.

One of the key strategies for heritage conservation is the integration of smart city technologies and innovations. By utilizing advanced digital tools, such as virtual reality and augmented reality, urban planners can create immersive experiences that allow residents and visitors to explore and appreciate historical sites. These technologies can also be used for educational purposes, enabling a deeper understanding of the significance of cultural heritage.

In addition, the development of urban transportation systems and infrastructure plays a crucial role in heritage conservation. By enhancing connectivity and accessibility to historical sites, urban planners can encourage more people to visit and appreciate these cultural treasures. This can be achieved through the construction of pedestrian-friendly streets, the expansion of public transportation networks, and the promotion of non-motorized transportation options.

Furthermore, vertical farming and urban agriculture can be integrated into Chinese urban planning as a means to preserve cultural heritage. By incorporating traditional farming practices and indigenous plant species into urban landscapes, urban planners can create green spaces that reflect the agricultural heritage of the region. This not only helps in conserving traditional knowledge and practices but also contributes to sustainable food production and enhances the resilience of urban ecosystems.

Additionally, eco-friendly and green building practices should be prioritized in new Chinese cities. By incorporating sustainable design principles, such as energy-efficient technologies and materials, urban planners can reduce the environmental impact of new constructions while preserving the historical character of the city. This can include retrofitting existing buildings with green technologies or designing new structures that blend harmoniously with the surrounding heritage buildings.

Finally, social and community development should be at the forefront of heritage conservation strategies. Engaging local communities in the preservation and promotion of cultural heritage can foster a sense of ownership and pride. This can be achieved through community-based initiatives, such as heritage festivals, workshops, and guided tours. By involving residents in the decision-making process, urban planners can ensure that heritage conservation efforts are inclusive and sustainable.

In conclusion, heritage conservation in Chinese cities requires a multi-faceted approach that integrates sustainable urban planning practices, cultural preservation initiatives, smart city technologies, and community engagement. By implementing these strategies, urban planners can contribute to the preservation of China's rich cultural heritage while promoting sustainable development and enhancing the quality of life for residents.

Balancing modernization and cultural preservation in new Chinese cities

In the rapid urbanization process that China has witnessed over the past few decades, the challenge of balancing modernization and cultural preservation has become increasingly important. As urban planners, it is crucial to find innovative solutions that allow for economic growth and development while also safeguarding the rich cultural heritage of Chinese cities.

Sustainable urban planning in Chinese cities has emerged as a key focus area for urban planners. By incorporating sustainable design principles, such as energy-efficient buildings, green spaces, and renewable energy sources, cities can reduce their carbon footprint and create a more environmentally friendly urban environment. However, it is essential to ensure that these sustainable practices do not overshadow or erode the cultural heritage of the city.

Cultural preservation and heritage conservation in new Chinese cities should be given equal importance alongside modernization efforts. Historic buildings and sites should be protected and integrated into the urban fabric, allowing residents and visitors to experience the city's cultural identity. Adaptive reuse of old buildings, such as transforming traditional hutongs into vibrant cultural and commercial spaces, can help preserve the past while embracing the future.

Smart city technologies and innovations play a significant role in Chinese urban development. These technologies can enhance the efficiency of urban transportation systems and infrastructure, making cities more livable and sustainable. However, it is vital to ensure that these technologies are implemented in a way that does not compromise the cultural heritage of the city. For example, smart transportation systems should be designed to complement the existing urban fabric rather than overshadowing or replacing traditional modes of transportation.

Vertical farming and urban agriculture have gained traction in Chinese urban planning. These practices not only contribute to food security but also promote sustainable living. Integrating vertical farms and urban agriculture into the cityscape can create a harmonious balance between modernization and cultural preservation, as they provide opportunities to reconnect with nature and traditional farming practices.

Eco-friendly and green building practices should be encouraged in new Chinese cities. By incorporating sustainable materials, energy-efficient systems, and green spaces, cities can reduce their environmental impact. However, it is crucial to ensure that these eco-friendly practices are sensitive to the local cultural context and do not compromise the architectural heritage of the city.

Social and community development in Chinese urban areas should be prioritized alongside economic development. Creating inclusive and vibrant communities that promote social cohesion and well-being is crucial for the long-term success of new Chinese cities. Urban planners should strive to create spaces that facilitate social interaction and cultural exchange, while also providing essential amenities and services for residents.

Urban resilience and disaster management are critical aspects of urban planning in Chinese cities. As cities face increasing climate risks and natural disasters, it is essential to develop strategies that enhance the resilience of urban areas. These strategies should take into account the cultural heritage of the city and incorporate traditional building techniques and knowledge to ensure the long-term protection of the city's cultural assets.

Urban poverty alleviation and inclusive growth strategies are fundamental to creating sustainable and equitable cities in China. Urban planners should design policies and interventions that address the needs of vulnerable populations and promote inclusive economic development. By providing access to affordable housing, education, healthcare, and job opportunities, cities can ensure that all residents can benefit from urbanization.

Urban design and architectural trends in new Chinese cities should reflect a balance between modernization and cultural preservation. By incorporating elements of traditional Chinese architecture and design principles into modern buildings and urban spaces, cities can create a unique sense of place that celebrates their cultural heritage while embracing the future.

In conclusion, as urban planners in new Chinese cities, the challenge lies in finding a delicate balance between modernization and cultural preservation. By incorporating sustainable practices, preserving cultural heritage, and promoting inclusive and resilient communities, we can create cities that are not only economically prosperous but also socially and culturally vibrant. Only by embracing this holistic approach can we truly shape the future of Chinese cities.

Chapter 4: Smart City Technologies and Innovations in Chinese Urban Development

Overview of smart city concepts and technologies

In recent years, the concept of smart cities has gained significant traction in the field of urban planning. As the world becomes increasingly urbanized, cities are facing numerous challenges such as population growth, resource scarcity, and environmental degradation. To address these issues, cities are turning to innovative technologies and concepts that can enhance their efficiency, sustainability, and livability. This subchapter provides an overview of smart city concepts and technologies that are being implemented in new Chinese cities.

Smart city technologies and innovations play a crucial role in Chinese urban development. These technologies leverage data, connectivity, and automation to improve the quality of life for residents, enhance urban services, and optimize resource utilization. For instance, the Internet of Things (IoT) is being utilized to create a network of interconnected devices and sensors that gather data on various aspects of urban life, such as traffic flow, energy consumption, and waste management. This data is then analyzed to make informed decisions and improve the efficiency of urban systems.

One area where smart city technologies are making a significant impact is in urban transportation systems and infrastructure. Chinese cities are adopting intelligent transportation systems that use real-time data to optimize traffic flow, reduce congestion, and enhance public transportation services. Additionally, the development of electric vehicles and smart charging infrastructure is helping to reduce emissions and improve air quality in Chinese cities.

Another important aspect of smart cities in China is vertical farming and urban agriculture. With limited arable land and an increasing demand for food, vertical farming allows for the cultivation of crops in vertical layers, utilizing space more efficiently. Furthermore, the integration of urban agriculture into smart city design not only provides fresh produce but also promotes sustainable and locally sourced food production.

Eco-friendly and green building practices are also gaining prominence in new Chinese cities. Buildings are being designed and constructed with energy-efficient materials, renewable energy systems, and advanced insulation techniques to minimize their environmental impact. Additionally, smart building management systems are being implemented to optimize energy consumption and improve occupant comfort.

As Chinese cities continue to grow, it is essential to prioritize social and community development. Smart city concepts can enhance citizen engagement, promote social inclusion, and improve the overall quality of life. For example, smart community platforms are being developed to facilitate communication between residents and local authorities, enabling them to voice their concerns and contribute to decision-making processes.

Furthermore, smart city technologies can enhance urban resilience and disaster management. By implementing early warning systems, real-time monitoring, and predictive analytics, cities can better respond to natural disasters and mitigate their impact. This is particularly important in a country prone to earthquakes, floods, and other natural hazards.

In conclusion, smart city concepts and technologies are transforming the way new Chinese cities are designed and developed. By leveraging data, connectivity, and automation, these cities are becoming more sustainable, efficient, and livable. From smart transportation systems to vertical farming and eco-friendly buildings, these innovations are shaping the future of urban planning in China. Moreover, they have the potential to address various challenges such as urban poverty, cultural preservation, and inclusive growth strategies. As urban planners, it is crucial to embrace these concepts and technologies to create cities that are not only smart but also inclusive, resilient, and sustainable.

Application of smart city technologies in Chinese urban development

As urban planners in China strive to create sustainable cities that preserve cultural heritage while incorporating innovative technologies, the application of smart city technologies has emerged as a crucial aspect of urban development. This subchapter delves into the various ways in which smart city technologies are being leveraged in Chinese cities, addressing the diverse needs and challenges faced by urban planners.

One of the key areas where smart city technologies are making a significant impact is sustainable urban planning. These technologies enable the integration of real-time data collection and analysis, allowing urban planners to make informed decisions about resource allocation, energy management, and waste reduction. By implementing smart grids, intelligent transportation systems, and energy-efficient buildings, Chinese cities are reducing their carbon footprint and striving towards a greener future.

Cultural preservation and heritage conservation are also important considerations in new Chinese cities. Smart city technologies are being employed to digitally preserve historical sites and artifacts, enabling virtual tours and interactive experiences for visitors. Furthermore, these technologies facilitate the efficient management and maintenance of cultural heritage, ensuring its longevity and accessibility for future generations.

In the realm of transportation, smart city technologies are revolutionizing urban mobility. Chinese cities are implementing intelligent traffic management systems, smart parking solutions, and electric vehicle charging infrastructure. These technologies not only enhance transportation efficiency but also contribute to a cleaner and more sustainable urban environment.

Another area where smart city technologies are being applied is in vertical farming and urban agriculture. As urban areas become more densely populated, the need for locally grown food is increasing. Smart farming technologies such as hydroponics, aquaponics, and vertical farming systems are being integrated into urban planning strategies, enabling the production of fresh and nutritious food within city limits.

Eco-friendly and green building practices are also gaining momentum in new Chinese cities. Smart city technologies are being utilized to monitor and optimize energy consumption, water usage, and waste management in buildings. This not only reduces environmental impact but also enhances the quality of life for residents.

Social and community development is another crucial aspect of urban planning in Chinese cities. Smart city technologies facilitate the creation of connected communities, enabling efficient delivery of public services, improved communication, and enhanced citizen participation. These technologies empower residents to actively engage in decision-making processes and contribute to the development of their neighborhoods.

In terms of urban resilience and disaster management, smart city technologies play a vital role in early warning systems, real-time monitoring of environmental conditions, and emergency response coordination. By harnessing the power of data and connectivity, Chinese cities are better equipped to mitigate the impact of natural disasters and ensure the safety of their residents.

Furthermore, smart city technologies are being leveraged to address urban poverty alleviation and inclusive growth strategies. By providing access to digital platforms, online education, and e-commerce opportunities, these technologies empower marginalized communities and promote economic development.

Finally, the subchapter explores the latest urban design and architectural trends in new Chinese cities. From sustainable skyscrapers and green rooftops to mixed-use developments and pedestrian-friendly streetscapes, smart city technologies are shaping the physical fabric of Chinese cities and creating vibrant and livable spaces for residents.

In conclusion, the application of smart city technologies in Chinese urban development is transforming the way cities are planned, built, and managed. By embracing these technologies, urban planners in China are creating sustainable, culturally rich, and technologically advanced cities that meet the diverse needs and aspirations of their residents.

Benefits and challenges of adopting smart city innovations in China

As urban planners, it is crucial to stay informed about the latest trends and innovations shaping the future of cities. One such trend that is rapidly gaining momentum in China is the adoption of smart city technologies and innovations. This subchapter aims to explore the benefits and challenges associated with this paradigm shift in Chinese urban development.

One of the primary benefits of adopting smart city innovations in China is the potential to improve the quality of life for its residents. Smart technologies can enhance various aspects of urban living, including transportation, energy management, waste management, and public safety. For example, the implementation of smart transportation systems can reduce traffic congestion and improve air quality, leading to a healthier and more sustainable urban environment.

Additionally, smart city innovations can contribute to sustainable urban planning in Chinese cities. By integrating data-driven solutions and

Internet of Things (IoT) technologies, urban planners can gain valuable insights into the usage patterns and needs of the city's residents. This data can inform decision-making processes and facilitate the development of more efficient and resource-conscious urban infrastructure.

Furthermore, the preservation of cultural heritage and the conservation of historic sites is a key concern in new Chinese cities. Smart city technologies can play a significant role in achieving this goal. For instance, the use of augmented reality and virtual reality can recreate historical sites and promote cultural tourism, while smart sensors can monitor and protect heritage buildings from potential damage or deterioration.

However, despite the many benefits, there are also challenges associated with the widespread adoption of smart city innovations in China. One major challenge is the sheer scale and complexity of implementing such technologies in existing urban environments. Retrofitting existing infrastructure and integrating various systems can be time-consuming and costly.

Another challenge is ensuring data privacy and cybersecurity in a connected city. With the increased reliance on data collection and sharing, there is a need to establish robust frameworks and regulations to protect the privacy of individuals and secure sensitive information from cyber threats.

Moreover, the digital divide and unequal access to technology can pose challenges in implementing smart city innovations. It is crucial to ensure that all segments of the population, including low-income communities, have equal access to the benefits of smart city technologies.

In conclusion, the adoption of smart city innovations in China presents numerous benefits, including improved quality of life, sustainable urban planning, and cultural preservation. However, challenges such as infrastructure retrofitting, data privacy, and digital divide must be addressed to fully harness the potential of these innovations. As urban planners, it is essential to navigate these challenges and embrace the opportunities offered by smart city technologies to create more sustainable, inclusive, and resilient cities in China.

Chapter 5: Urban Transportation Systems and Infrastructure in New Chinese Cities

Evolution of transportation systems in Chinese cities

Introduction:

Transportation systems play a vital role in shaping the development and sustainability of urban areas. In the context of China, rapid urbanization and economic growth have presented unique challenges and opportunities for the evolution of transportation systems in its cities. This subchapter explores the historical trajectory and future trends in transportation systems in Chinese cities, with a focus on sustainable urban planning, cultural preservation, smart city technologies, and urban infrastructure.

Historical Context:

The evolution of transportation systems in Chinese cities can be traced back to ancient times when cities were connected by canals and waterways. As urbanization progressed, the focus shifted towards land-based transportation systems, including the construction of roads and bridges. With the advent of industrialization, the introduction of railways and later highways revolutionized transportation in China.

Sustainable Urban Planning:

Recognizing the challenges posed by rapid urbanization, Chinese cities have embraced sustainable urban planning principles to mitigate traffic congestion, reduce air pollution, and promote energy efficiency. This has led to the extensive development of public transportation systems, including the expansion of subway networks, the introduction of electric buses, and the promotion of cycling infrastructure.

Cultural Preservation and Heritage Conservation:

Chinese cities have also made efforts to integrate cultural preservation and heritage conservation into their transportation systems. This includes the preservation of historic buildings, the incorporation of traditional architectural elements in transport infrastructure, and the development of pedestrian-friendly streetscapes that showcase local culture and traditions.

Smart City Technologies and Innovations:

China has emerged as a global leader in the adoption of smart city technologies to enhance transportation systems. This includes the use of advanced data analytics, artificial intelligence, and Internet of Things (IoT) devices to optimize traffic flow, improve public transportation services, and enhance the overall efficiency of urban mobility.

Urban Transportation Systems and Infrastructure:

The evolution of transportation systems in Chinese cities has also been characterized by the development of state-of-the-art urban transportation infrastructure. This includes the construction of high-speed rail networks that connect major cities, the expansion of airports and seaports, and the implementation of intelligent transportation systems that enable seamless connectivity and interoperability.

Conclusion:

The evolution of transportation systems in Chinese cities reflects a commitment to sustainable urban planning, cultural preservation, and the integration of smart city technologies. As Chinese cities continue to grow and face new challenges, it is crucial for urban planners to leverage these trends and innovations to create efficient, resilient, and inclusive transportation systems that cater to the diverse needs of their inhabitants. By prioritizing sustainability, cultural heritage, and technological advancements, Chinese cities can pave the way for a future where transportation is not only efficient but also environmentally friendly, socially inclusive, and economically vibrant.

Current transportation infrastructure in new Chinese cities

The rapid urbanization in China has led to the development of new cities that require modern and efficient transportation infrastructure to cater to the growing population. This subchapter will provide an overview of the current transportation infrastructure in new Chinese cities, highlighting the efforts made towards sustainable urban planning, cultural preservation, and the adoption of smart city technologies.

Sustainable urban planning in Chinese cities has become a priority, with a focus on reducing carbon emissions and promoting eco-friendly transportation options. New Chinese cities have implemented comprehensive public transportation systems, including buses, trams, and subway networks. These systems are designed to be accessible and convenient, encouraging residents to rely less on private vehicles.

Cultural preservation and heritage conservation are integral aspects of urban development in China. Many new cities have incorporated traditional architectural styles and preserved historical landmarks, creating a sense of cultural identity. Transportation infrastructure has been carefully planned to ensure the preservation of cultural heritage sites, with dedicated routes and pedestrian-friendly areas.

Smart city technologies and innovations play a crucial role in the transportation infrastructure of new Chinese cities. Advanced systems, such as intelligent traffic management, real-time data analysis, and smart parking, have been implemented to improve traffic flow and reduce congestion. Additionally, electronic payment systems and mobile applications have been introduced to enhance the convenience of public transportation.

Urban transportation systems in new Chinese cities also prioritize efficiency and connectivity. High-speed rail networks have been established, connecting cities and reducing travel time. Intermodal transportation hubs have been constructed, integrating various modes of transportation, including buses, trains, and bicycles, to provide seamless connectivity for commuters.

To promote sustainable and green practices, new Chinese cities have also invested in electric and hybrid vehicles. Charging stations have been installed throughout the city, encouraging the adoption of eco-friendly transportation options. Additionally, bicycle-sharing programs have been implemented, providing an alternative mode of transportation for short-distance travel.

In conclusion, the current transportation infrastructure in new Chinese cities reflects a commitment to sustainable urban planning, cultural preservation, and the adoption of smart city technologies. The integration of efficient public transportation systems, preservation of cultural heritage sites, implementation of smart city technologies, and promotion of eco-friendly transportation options have contributed to the overall development and livability of these cities. As urban planners continue to design and develop new Chinese cities, they must consider the importance of a well-connected and sustainable transportation infrastructure to ensure a prosperous and resilient future.

Future trends and innovations in urban transportation in China

Future trends and innovations in urban transportation in China are of great interest to urban planners, as they play a crucial role in shaping the development of new Chinese cities. With the rapid urbanization taking place in the country, there is a need for sustainable and efficient transportation systems that can accommodate the growing population and address the challenges of congestion, pollution, and limited space.

One of the key trends in urban transportation in China is the promotion of electric vehicles (EVs). The government has been actively supporting the adoption of EVs by offering subsidies and implementing policies to encourage their use. As a result, China has become the world's largest market for EVs, with a significant increase in the number of charging stations across the country. This trend is expected to continue in the future, with more advancements in battery technology and the development of smart charging infrastructure.

Another trend is the integration of public transportation systems, such as buses, metro, and light rail, to provide seamless and efficient travel options for commuters. The use of smart technology, such as real-time data and mobile apps, has made it easier for passengers to plan their journeys and access different modes of transportation. Additionally, the introduction of shared mobility services, such as bike-sharing and car-sharing, has further enhanced the accessibility and convenience of urban transportation.

In terms of infrastructure, China is investing heavily in the development of high-speed rail networks, which are not only efficient but also environmentally friendly. These networks connect major cities, reducing travel time and relieving the pressure on air and road transportation. The integration of high-speed rail with other modes of transportation, such as airports and metro systems, is also being explored to create an interconnected and multimodal transportation network.

Furthermore, the concept of smart cities is gaining momentum in China, with the integration of various technologies to improve the efficiency and sustainability of urban transportation. This includes the use of sensors and intelligent traffic management systems to monitor and optimize traffic flow, as well as the development of autonomous vehicles and intelligent transportation systems.

In conclusion, future trends and innovations in urban transportation in China are focused on sustainability, efficiency, and integration. The promotion of electric vehicles, the integration of public transportation systems, the development of high-speed rail networks, and the implementation of smart city technologies are all contributing to the transformation of urban transportation in China. As urban planners, it is essential to stay updated with these trends and incorporate them into the planning and design of new Chinese cities to create sustainable and livable urban environments.

Chapter 6: Vertical Farming and Urban Agriculture in Chinese Urban Planning

Importance of urban agriculture in sustainable development

Urban agriculture plays a crucial role in the sustainable development of cities, providing a multitude of social, economic, environmental, and health benefits. As urban planners, it is essential to recognize the importance of incorporating urban agriculture into our designs and strategies for new Chinese cities.

Sustainable urban planning in Chinese cities can greatly benefit from the integration of urban agriculture. By incorporating green spaces and agricultural areas within the cityscape, we can create a more balanced and sustainable environment. Urban agriculture promotes biodiversity, improves air quality, and reduces the urban heat island effect. It also helps mitigate climate change by absorbing carbon dioxide, reducing energy consumption, and promoting sustainable water management practices.

Cultural preservation and heritage conservation in new Chinese cities can be enhanced through urban agriculture. By reviving traditional farming practices and incorporating them into the urban fabric, we can reconnect people with their cultural heritage. Urban agriculture can serve as a means to preserve traditional crops, farming techniques, and knowledge, ensuring the continuity of cultural traditions for future generations.

Smart city technologies and innovations in Chinese urban development can be integrated into urban agriculture practices. Utilizing smart sensors, data analytics, and automation, we can optimize resource usage, monitor plant health, and improve overall efficiency. This integration can lead to higher crop yields, reduced water consumption, and improved food security for urban populations.

Urban transportation systems and infrastructure in new Chinese cities can benefit from urban agriculture. By locating urban farms near residential areas, we can reduce the distance food needs to travel, minimizing transportation-related carbon emissions. This localized approach to food production also reduces the strain on existing transportation systems and improves food accessibility for urban residents.

Vertical farming and urban agriculture can be integrated into Chinese urban planning to maximize land use efficiency. With limited available land in urban areas, vertical farming offers a sustainable solution by utilizing vertical space. This innovative approach allows for year-round crop production, reduced water usage, and the ability to grow food in close proximity to consumers.

Eco-friendly and green building practices in new Chinese cities can be complemented by urban agriculture. By incorporating green roofs, vertical gardens, and rooftop farms, we can enhance the environmental performance of buildings. These green spaces not only improve air quality and reduce energy consumption but also provide opportunities for urban residents to engage in food production and connect with nature.

Social and community development in Chinese urban areas can be fostered through urban agriculture. Community gardens and urban farms serve as gathering spaces, fostering social interaction, and strengthening community bonds. Urban agriculture also provides opportunities for education, job creation, and skill development, benefiting local residents and promoting social inclusion.

Urban resilience and disaster management in new Chinese cities can be enhanced by urban agriculture. By diversifying food sources and reducing dependence on external food supply chains, cities become more resilient to disruptions. Urban agriculture can also contribute to disaster management strategies by providing emergency food supplies and supporting food relief efforts during times of crisis.

Urban poverty alleviation and inclusive growth strategies in Chinese cities can be supported by urban agriculture. By providing opportunities for small-scale farming and entrepreneurship, urban agriculture can empower marginalized communities and contribute to poverty reduction. It also offers a source of affordable, fresh produce, improving food security and nutrition for low-income urban residents.

Urban design and architectural trends in new Chinese cities can be enriched by the integration of urban agriculture. By incorporating green spaces, rooftop gardens, and vertical farms into architectural designs, we create visually appealing and sustainable urban environments. The integration of nature into the built environment enhances the quality of life for urban residents and promotes overall well-being.

In conclusion, urban agriculture plays a crucial role in the sustainable development of Chinese cities. As urban planners, it is imperative to recognize and prioritize the importance of urban agriculture in our designs and strategies. By incorporating urban agriculture into our plans, we can create more sustainable, resilient, and inclusive cities that prioritize the well-being of both people and the environment.

Vertical farming techniques and their application in Chinese cities

As urban planners, it is imperative to explore sustainable urban planning solutions that can address the growing challenges of food security and environmental degradation in Chinese cities. One innovative approach that has gained attention in recent years is vertical farming. This subchapter will delve into the various techniques of vertical farming and their potential application in Chinese cities.

Vertical farming is a revolutionary concept that involves cultivating crops in vertically stacked layers, using controlled environment agriculture (CEA) technology. This technique maximizes the use of limited urban space by growing crops in high-rise buildings or skyscrapers, completely eliminating the need for expansive farmland.

One technique commonly used in vertical farming is hydroponics, which involves growing plants in nutrient-rich water solutions, without soil. This method allows for precise control of nutrient levels, water usage, and the elimination of pesticides, resulting in higher crop yields and reduced environmental impact. Another technique is aeroponics, which involves growing plants in a mist environment without soil or water. This technique reduces water usage by up to 95% compared to traditional farming methods.

Chinese cities can greatly benefit from the implementation of vertical farming techniques. With rapid urbanization and limited arable land, vertical farming offers a sustainable solution to meet the increasing demand for fresh, locally grown produce. By bringing agriculture closer to urban areas, it reduces transportation costs and carbon emissions associated with long-distance food supply chains.

Furthermore, vertical farming promotes cultural preservation and heritage conservation in new Chinese cities. By integrating traditional agricultural practices and local crops into vertical farming systems, cities can maintain their cultural identity while embracing modern technology.

To support the adoption of vertical farming, smart city technologies and innovations can be utilized. The integration of sensors, automation, and artificial intelligence can optimize resource usage, monitor plant health, and improve overall efficiency.

In conclusion, vertical farming techniques hold great promise for sustainable urban planning in Chinese cities. By utilizing hydroponics, aeroponics, and other CEA technologies, cities can address food security, environmental degradation, and cultural preservation simultaneously. By embracing smart city technologies and innovations, Chinese cities can lead the way in urban agriculture and create a more resilient and sustainable future.

Integration of urban agriculture in Chinese urban planning

Urban agriculture, the practice of cultivating crops and raising animals within urban areas, has gained significant attention in recent years due to its numerous social, environmental, and economic benefits. In the context of Chinese cities, which are undergoing rapid urbanization and facing challenges such as food security, pollution, and limited green spaces, the integration of urban agriculture in urban planning has emerged as a promising solution.

Sustainable urban planning in Chinese cities recognizes the importance of incorporating urban agriculture as a key component. By allocating spaces for community gardens, rooftop farms, and vertical farming systems, cities can promote local food production, reduce carbon emissions from transportation, and enhance the overall sustainability of urban environments. Additionally, urban agriculture contributes to the preservation of cultural heritage by reviving traditional farming practices and reconnecting urban dwellers with their agricultural roots.

Smart city technologies and innovations in Chinese urban development play a crucial role in the integration of urban agriculture. By leveraging advanced systems such as hydroponics, aquaponics, and automated vertical farming, cities can optimize resource utilization, monitor crop growth, and mitigate potential risks. These technologies enable efficient food production in limited spaces, ensuring high yields while minimizing water and energy consumption.

Urban transportation systems and infrastructure in new Chinese cities need to consider the integration of urban agriculture. Transportation networks should facilitate the distribution of locally grown produce from urban farms to consumers. This not only reduces reliance on long-distance transportation but also promotes the consumption of fresh and nutritious food, leading to improved public health outcomes.

Furthermore, the concept of vertical farming and urban agriculture in Chinese urban planning aligns with eco-friendly and green building practices. Integrating green roofs, living walls, and urban farms into building designs can enhance energy efficiency, improve air quality, and create urban ecosystems that support biodiversity. These eco-friendly practices contribute to the overall sustainability and resilience of Chinese cities.

Social and community development in Chinese urban areas can be fostered through urban agriculture. Involving local residents in the cultivation and maintenance of urban farms creates a strong sense of community ownership and promotes social cohesion. Moreover, urban agriculture can provide employment opportunities and skill development for marginalized populations, contributing to urban poverty alleviation and inclusive growth strategies.

To ensure the success and resilience of urban agriculture, urban planners need to consider disaster management and urban resilience in Chinese cities. By integrating urban agriculture into disaster preparedness plans, cities can enhance their ability to respond to food shortages and ensure food security during emergencies.

In conclusion, the integration of urban agriculture in Chinese urban planning offers a holistic approach to address various challenges faced by Chinese cities. By embracing sustainable practices, leveraging smart technologies, and fostering community engagement, urban agriculture can contribute to the creation of vibrant, resilient, and inclusive cities in China.

Chapter 7: Eco-friendly and Green Building Practices in New Chinese Cities

Green building principles and certifications

Green building principles and certifications play a crucial role in shaping the future of Chinese cities. As urban planners, it is essential to understand the significance of integrating sustainable practices into the design and construction of buildings. This subchapter will explore the key principles and certifications associated with green building in China, providing valuable insights for urban planners who are committed to building a more sustainable and resilient future.

Sustainable urban planning in Chinese cities requires a holistic approach that considers the environmental, social, and economic aspects of development. One of the fundamental principles of green building is minimizing the environmental impact by reducing energy consumption, conserving water, and promoting the use of renewable resources. This can be achieved through various strategies, such as the efficient use of materials, incorporating renewable energy technologies, and implementing water-saving measures.

In China, several certifications have been developed to recognize buildings that meet specific sustainability criteria. One of the most well-known certifications is the Leadership in Energy and Environmental Design (LEED) certification, which is widely used globally. LEED evaluates buildings based on categories such as energy efficiency, water efficiency, indoor environmental quality, and sustainable site development. Another notable certification is the China Green Building Label, which is specific to the Chinese context and evaluates buildings based on criteria tailored to local environmental conditions and cultural considerations.

These certifications not only ensure that buildings are environmentally friendly but also provide numerous benefits for occupants and the wider community. Green buildings offer healthier indoor environments, improved air quality, and enhanced comfort for occupants. They also contribute to reducing greenhouse gas emissions, mitigating climate change, and conserving natural resources.

As urban planners, it is crucial to familiarize ourselves with these certifications and encourage their adoption in Chinese cities. By incorporating green building principles and pursuing certifications, we can create more sustainable and resilient urban environments that address the challenges of rapid urbanization, while also preserving cultural heritage and promoting social and community development.

In conclusion, green building principles and certifications are essential components of sustainable urban planning in Chinese cities. By integrating these practices into the design and construction of buildings, we can create more environmentally friendly, energy-efficient, and resilient cities. As urban planners, it is our responsibility to advocate for the adoption of green building principles and promote the use of certifications to ensure a sustainable future for Chinese cities.

Adoption of eco-friendly building practices in Chinese cities

Introduction:

In recent years, China has experienced rapid urbanization, resulting in the construction of numerous new cities. This chapter explores the adoption of eco-friendly building practices in Chinese cities and their significance for sustainable urban planning, cultural preservation, smart city technologies, transportation systems, vertical farming, and community development. It also addresses the importance of eco-friendly practices in disaster management, poverty alleviation, and urban design trends.

Sustainable Urban Planning in Chinese Cities:

As the urban population continues to grow, it is crucial to integrate sustainable practices in urban planning. Eco-friendly building practices, such as green roofs, rainwater harvesting, and energy-efficient design, can reduce the environmental impact of new cities. By incorporating green spaces and promoting walkability, Chinese cities can create sustainable and livable urban environments.

Cultural Preservation and Heritage Conservation in New Chinese Cities:

China's rich cultural heritage and historical sites must be protected amidst rapid urban development. Eco-friendly building practices can play a crucial role in preserving cultural heritage by integrating traditional architectural elements, using locally sourced materials, and adapting to the surrounding landscape. This approach ensures the continuity of cultural identity and heritage in new Chinese cities.

Smart City Technologies and Innovations in Chinese Urban Development:

Eco-friendly building practices align perfectly with the goals of smart city development. By incorporating smart technologies, such as energy management systems, smart grids, and intelligent waste management, Chinese cities can enhance their sustainability and efficiency. These technologies not only reduce environmental impact but also improve the quality of life for residents.

Urban Transportation Systems and Infrastructure in New Chinese Cities:

Eco-friendly building practices extend beyond the construction of buildings. They also encompass the development of sustainable transportation systems and infrastructure. Chinese cities can promote the use of electric vehicles, build bike-friendly infrastructure, and invest in public transportation to reduce carbon emissions and alleviate traffic congestion.

Vertical Farming and Urban Agriculture in Chinese Urban Planning:

To address food security and promote self-sufficiency, vertical farming and urban agriculture can be integrated into eco-friendly building practices. By utilizing rooftop gardens, hydroponic systems, and community gardens, Chinese cities can produce fresh and healthy food locally, reducing the reliance on long-distance transportation and minimizing the carbon footprint.

Conclusion:

The adoption of eco-friendly building practices in Chinese cities is of paramount importance to achieve sustainable urban development. It not only contributes to environmental conservation but also supports cultural preservation, smart city innovations, efficient transportation systems, urban agriculture, and community development. By embracing these practices, Chinese cities can become models of sustainable urban planning and design, ensuring a better future for both people and the planet.

Case studies of successful green buildings in China

China has made significant strides in recent years towards sustainable urban planning and the development of green buildings. These innovative structures not only reduce the environmental impact of urban areas but also improve the quality of life for residents. In this subchapter, we will explore several case studies of successful green buildings in China that have become models for sustainable urban development.

One outstanding example is the Shanghai Tower, located in the heart of Shanghai's Lujiazui Financial District. This supertall skyscraper stands at a staggering 632 meters and is the second-tallest building in the world. The Shanghai Tower incorporates numerous green building features, including a double-skin façade that provides insulation and reduces energy consumption. The tower also utilizes rainwater harvesting and greywater recycling systems, reducing water usage by 40%. These innovative design elements have earned the Shanghai Tower LEED Platinum certification, making it a shining example of eco-friendly building practices.

Another noteworthy case study is the Crystal Island project in Moscow, which was designed by the Chinese architectural firm, MAD Architects. This ambitious project aims to create a self-sustaining city within a building, with a focus on energy efficiency and environmental conservation. The Crystal Island features a unique, biomimetic design inspired by the shape of a snowflake, which allows for maximum natural light penetration and reduces the need for artificial lighting. The building also incorporates wind turbines and solar panels to generate renewable energy, making it a model for sustainable urban planning and design.

In addition to these large-scale projects, China has also seen the emergence of smaller, community-based green buildings. One such example is the Vertical Forest in Nanjing, designed by Italian architect Stefano Boeri. This innovative residential complex features over 1,000 trees and 2,500 cascading plants, which help to improve air quality and reduce carbon dioxide emissions. The Vertical Forest has become a symbol of sustainable urban development, showcasing how green building practices can be integrated into high-density urban areas.

These case studies of successful green buildings in China demonstrate the country's commitment to sustainable urban planning and design. By incorporating innovative technologies and eco-friendly practices, these buildings not only reduce environmental impact but also create healthier and more livable spaces for residents. As urban planners, it is crucial to learn from these examples and integrate green building practices into future urban development projects in China. By doing so, we can create sustainable, resilient, and inclusive cities that prioritize the well-being of both people and the planet.

Chapter 8: Social and Community Development in Chinese Urban Areas

Importance of social and community development in urban areas

In the fast-paced development of new Chinese cities, it is crucial to prioritize social and community development as a key aspect of sustainable urban planning. As urban planners, we have the responsibility to create spaces that not only fulfill the physical needs of the residents but also foster a sense of community, cultural preservation, and inclusivity.

One of the primary reasons why social and community development is essential in urban areas is the promotion of sustainable urban planning in Chinese cities. By creating neighborhoods and communities that encourage social interactions and a sense of belonging, we can reduce the reliance on private vehicles and promote walkability and public transportation. This, in turn, helps to reduce air pollution, traffic congestion, and carbon emissions, contributing to a more sustainable and livable city.

Furthermore, cultural preservation and heritage conservation in new Chinese cities can be achieved through social and community development. By integrating cultural elements and historical structures into the urban fabric, we can create a sense of place and identity for the residents. This not only preserves the rich heritage of the city but also attracts tourists, boosting the local economy.

Smart city technologies and innovations in Chinese urban development can also be enhanced through social and community development. By building strong social networks and community engagement platforms, we can leverage technology to improve governance, service delivery, and citizen participation. This creates a more inclusive and participatory decision-making process, ultimately leading to better urban planning outcomes.

Another reason to prioritize social and community development is its impact on urban resilience and disaster management in new Chinese cities. By fostering strong community ties and social networks, we can enhance disaster preparedness and response. In times of crisis, a well-connected community can provide support, share resources, and coordinate relief efforts more effectively.

Lastly, social and community development plays a vital role in urban poverty alleviation and inclusive growth strategies in Chinese cities. By providing affordable housing, community facilities, and access to education and healthcare, we can reduce inequalities and promote social mobility. This creates a more equitable and inclusive city where everyone has the opportunity to thrive.

In conclusion, social and community development is of utmost importance in new Chinese cities. By prioritizing sustainable urban planning, cultural preservation, smart city technologies, urban resilience, poverty alleviation, and inclusive growth, we can create cities that are not only environmentally sustainable but also socially vibrant and inclusive for all residents. As urban planners, it is our duty to design the future of Chinese cities with a focus on social and community development.

Strategies for promoting social cohesion in Chinese cities

Social cohesion is crucial for the sustainable development of Chinese cities. It refers to the sense of belonging, trust, and cooperation among diverse groups of people living in urban areas. To ensure social cohesion, urban planners must adopt effective strategies that promote inclusivity, cultural preservation, community development, and equitable growth. This subchapter explores various approaches to achieving social cohesion in Chinese cities.

1. Creating inclusive public spaces: Designing public spaces that are accessible, safe, and welcoming to people from all walks of life fosters social interaction and community bonding. Urban planners can incorporate features such as parks, community centers, and pedestrian-friendly streets to encourage people to come together.

2. Preserving cultural heritage: Chinese cities have a rich cultural heritage that must be preserved and celebrated. Urban planners should prioritize the protection of historical sites, traditional neighborhoods, and cultural landmarks. This can be achieved through adaptive reuse, restoration projects, and the integration of cultural elements in new developments.

3. Leveraging smart city technologies: Smart city technologies can play a significant role in promoting social cohesion. For instance, digital platforms can be used to facilitate community engagement, citizen participation, and the sharing of resources. These technologies can bridge the gap between different social groups and facilitate communication and collaboration.

4. Developing sustainable transportation systems: Efficient and accessible transportation systems are vital for social cohesion. Urban planners should prioritize the development of public transportation networks, cycling infrastructure, and pedestrian-friendly streets. These measures promote social interaction, reduce congestion, and improve air quality.

5. Introducing vertical farming and urban agriculture: Promoting urban agriculture initiatives and vertical farming can enhance community engagement and social cohesion. These initiatives provide opportunities for people to come together, learn new skills, and contribute to local food production. They also promote sustainable and self-sufficient neighborhoods.

6. Encouraging eco-friendly building practices: Green building practices contribute to social cohesion by creating healthier and more sustainable living environments. Urban planners should advocate for energy-efficient buildings, green spaces, and the use of renewable materials. These practices improve the quality of life, promote community well-being, and reduce the carbon footprint.

7. Facilitating social and community development: Urban planners should focus on creating mixed-use developments that integrate residential, commercial, and recreational facilities. The provision of amenities such as schools, healthcare centers, and community centers fosters social interaction, enhances community cohesion, and contributes to the overall well-being of residents.

8. Building urban resilience and disaster management: Urban planners must prioritize the resilience of Chinese cities to natural disasters and other crises. This involves incorporating disaster-resistant infrastructure, early warning systems, and emergency response mechanisms. An emphasis on social cohesion during times of crisis can help communities recover and rebuild more effectively.

9. Implementing inclusive growth strategies: Urban poverty alleviation and inclusive growth strategies are essential for reducing social disparities and ensuring social cohesion. Urban planners should focus on creating economic opportunities, affordable housing, and social welfare programs that benefit all segments of society.

10. Embracing innovative urban design and architectural trends: Urban planners should stay updated on the latest trends in urban design and architecture to create cities that are vibrant, livable, and socially cohesive. This includes embracing sustainable design principles, mixed-use developments, and innovative housing solutions that accommodate diverse lifestyles.

In conclusion, promoting social cohesion in Chinese cities requires a multifaceted approach that encompasses inclusive public spaces, cultural preservation, smart city technologies, sustainable transportation, urban agriculture, eco-friendly building practices, social and community development, urban resilience, inclusive growth strategies, and innovative urban design. By adopting these strategies, urban planners can create cities that are socially inclusive, culturally vibrant, and sustainable for future generations.

Community engagement and participation in urban planning processes

Community engagement and participation in urban planning processes play a crucial role in shaping the future of Chinese cities. As urban planners, it is essential to involve the community in decision-making processes to ensure sustainable development, cultural preservation, and the well-being of residents.

Sustainable urban planning in Chinese cities requires active community participation. By engaging citizens in the planning process, urban planners can tap into local knowledge, needs, and aspirations. This collaborative approach ensures that urban development is not only environmentally friendly but also meets the social and economic needs of the community. Through community engagement, planners can identify sustainable practices and innovative solutions that align with the unique characteristics of each city.

Cultural preservation and heritage conservation in new Chinese cities also rely heavily on community engagement. The participation of local residents, historians, and cultural experts is vital in identifying and protecting cultural assets and heritage sites. By involving the community, planners can ensure that development projects respect and integrate traditional architectural styles, cultural practices, and historic landmarks. This approach not only preserves the city's identity but also enhances its appeal to tourists and promotes cultural tourism.

Smart city technologies and innovations in Chinese urban development can greatly benefit from community engagement. By involving citizens in the design and implementation of smart city initiatives, planners can ensure that technology meets the needs and preferences of the community. Engaging residents in the decision-making process fosters a sense of ownership and responsibility, leading to more effective and sustainable smart city solutions.

Urban transportation systems and infrastructure in new Chinese cities can be greatly improved through community engagement. By involving residents in the planning and design of transportation systems, planners can ensure that they meet the needs of all citizens, including those with disabilities and limited mobility. Community input can also help identify areas in need of improved infrastructure, such as bike lanes, pedestrian walkways, and public transportation hubs, ultimately promoting sustainable and inclusive urban mobility.

Vertical farming and urban agriculture in Chinese urban planning can benefit from community engagement to ensure successful implementation. By involving residents in the planning and management of urban agriculture projects, planners can promote food security, environmental sustainability, and community development. Engagement initiatives can include community gardens, rooftop farming, and educational programs that empower residents to grow their own food and embrace sustainable agricultural practices.

Eco-friendly and green building practices in new Chinese cities can be better understood and embraced through community engagement. By involving residents, architects, and developers in the design and construction process, planners can ensure that green buildings meet the needs and preferences of the community. Engaging residents in sustainable building initiatives can also promote awareness and participation in energy-saving practices, waste reduction, and green living.

Social and community development in Chinese urban areas can be enhanced through community engagement. By involving residents in the planning and implementation of social programs and community spaces, planners can create inclusive and vibrant neighborhoods. Engaging citizens can help identify the specific needs of different communities, such as childcare facilities, recreational areas, and healthcare services, ultimately fostering social cohesion and well-being.

Urban resilience and disaster management in new Chinese cities require the active participation of the community. By involving residents in disaster preparedness initiatives, planners can ensure that cities are well-equipped to face natural disasters and other emergencies. Engaging citizens in resilience planning can include community training programs, early warning systems, and the development of safe havens, ultimately promoting the well-being and safety of residents.

Urban poverty alleviation and inclusive growth strategies in Chinese cities can be better addressed through community engagement. By involving residents, community leaders, and social workers in poverty alleviation programs, planners can identify and address the root causes of urban poverty. Engaging citizens can also foster entrepreneurship and employment opportunities, promoting inclusive and sustainable economic growth.

Urban design and architectural trends in new Chinese cities can be better understood and embraced through community engagement. By involving residents in the design process, planners can create cities that reflect the aspirations and cultural values of the community. Engaging citizens in urban design initiatives can also promote a sense of pride and ownership, leading to well-maintained public spaces and a more attractive urban environment.

In conclusion, community engagement and participation in urban planning processes are essential for sustainable, inclusive, and culturally sensitive development in Chinese cities. By involving the community, planners can tap into local knowledge, preserve cultural heritage, promote smart city technologies, improve transportation systems, enhance urban agriculture, embrace eco-friendly practices, foster social development, ensure resilience, alleviate poverty, and create aesthetically pleasing cities that residents can be proud of.

Chapter 9: Urban Resilience and Disaster Management in New Chinese Cities

Understanding urban resilience and its relevance in Chinese cities

Urban resilience is a concept that has gained significant attention in recent years, and its relevance in Chinese cities cannot be overstated. As China rapidly urbanizes and faces numerous challenges, including climate change, natural disasters, and social and economic volatility, building resilient cities has become a critical goal for urban planners.

Chinese cities are particularly vulnerable to various risks due to their size, population density, and geographic location. For instance, coastal cities like Shanghai are at risk of rising sea levels and extreme weather events, while inland cities like Chengdu face threats of earthquakes and water scarcity. Therefore, understanding urban resilience is crucial to effectively addressing these challenges and ensuring the long-term sustainability of Chinese cities.

Resilience refers to the ability of a city to bounce back and recover quickly from shocks and stresses. It involves developing strategies and implementing measures to strengthen infrastructures, enhance social cohesion, and protect natural resources. By fostering resilience, Chinese cities can better withstand and adapt to the challenges they face, ultimately improving the quality of life for their residents.

In the context of sustainable urban planning in Chinese cities, urban resilience plays a vital role. It requires incorporating principles of sustainability, such as efficient resource management, renewable energy, and green infrastructure, into city planning and design. By integrating these practices, cities can reduce their vulnerability to environmental risks and promote sustainable development.

Furthermore, urban resilience intersects with cultural preservation and heritage conservation in new Chinese cities. Cultural heritage sites often face threats from urban development and natural disasters. Therefore, it is crucial to incorporate resilience measures that protect these valuable assets while ensuring their preservation for future generations.

Smart city technologies and innovations also contribute to urban resilience by enhancing the efficiency and effectiveness of urban systems. Through the use of data analytics, sensor networks, and artificial intelligence, cities can monitor and respond to disasters more effectively, improve transportation systems, and optimize resource management.

Moreover, urban resilience is closely tied to disaster management. Chinese cities experience a range of hazards, including earthquakes, floods, and typhoons. By developing robust disaster management plans, cities can better respond to emergencies, minimize damage, and protect lives.

In conclusion, understanding urban resilience and its relevance in Chinese cities is crucial for urban planners. It encompasses various aspects, including sustainable urban planning, cultural preservation, smart city technologies, disaster management, and more. By incorporating resilience into city planning and design, Chinese cities can better navigate the challenges they face, promote sustainable development, and improve the quality of life for their residents.

Disaster management strategies in new Chinese cities

In recent years, the rapid urbanization in China has brought about numerous challenges, including the need for effective disaster management strategies in new cities. With the increased frequency and intensity of natural disasters such as earthquakes, floods, and typhoons, it has become crucial for urban planners to develop comprehensive plans to mitigate the impact of these events. This subchapter will explore the various disaster management strategies implemented in new Chinese cities, addressing the concerns of urban planners and the niches of sustainable urban planning, cultural preservation, smart city technologies, urban transportation, vertical farming, eco-friendly building practices, social and community development, urban resilience, urban poverty alleviation, and architectural trends.

One of the key strategies in disaster management in new Chinese cities is the integration of smart city technologies. By leveraging the power of data analytics and Internet of Things (IoT) devices, urban planners can monitor and respond to disasters in real-time. For example, sensors can provide early warning systems for earthquakes or floods, enabling authorities to evacuate residents promptly. Additionally, urban transportation systems play a vital role in disaster management, as efficient evacuation routes and emergency response plans must be in place. This subchapter will delve into the innovative transportation infrastructure being implemented in new Chinese cities, such as intelligent traffic management systems and the use of drones for emergency medical supplies delivery.

Furthermore, disaster management strategies in new Chinese cities must incorporate sustainable urban planning practices. This includes the implementation of eco-friendly and green building practices, such as the use of renewable energy sources and the integration of green spaces into urban designs. Vertical farming and urban agriculture can also contribute to disaster resilience by ensuring a steady supply of food during emergencies.

In terms of social and community development, disaster management strategies should focus on building resilient communities that are prepared to respond and recover from disasters. This can involve training programs, community-based early warning systems, and the establishment of community centers equipped with emergency supplies.

Overall, this subchapter will provide urban planners with valuable insights into the disaster management strategies being implemented in new Chinese cities. By adopting a multidisciplinary approach that integrates sustainable urban planning, smart city technologies, and community development, China is paving the way for effective disaster resilience and management in the face of rapid urbanization.

Building resilience against natural and man-made disasters in urban areas

Introduction:

In recent years, Chinese cities have experienced rapid urbanization, resulting in increased vulnerability to natural and man-made disasters. As urban planners, it is imperative to design and implement strategies that enhance resilience and mitigate the impacts of these disasters. This subchapter will explore various approaches to building resilience in Chinese cities, focusing on sustainable urban planning, cultural preservation, smart city technologies, transportation systems, vertical farming, eco-friendly building practices, social development, disaster management, poverty alleviation, and urban design trends.

Sustainable Urban Planning in Chinese Cities:

Sustainable urban planning plays a crucial role in building resilience against disasters. By integrating green spaces, improving waste management systems, and promoting renewable energy sources, Chinese cities can become more resilient to climate-related disasters such as flooding and heatwaves. Additionally, sustainable urban planning should prioritize reducing carbon emissions and promoting energy-efficient practices to mitigate the impact of man-made disasters.

Cultural Preservation and Heritage Conservation in New Chinese Cities:

Preserving cultural heritage is essential for building resilience in Chinese cities. By recognizing the value of historical buildings and neighborhoods, urban planners can ensure the preservation of cultural identity and promote community resilience. Integrating traditional architectural elements into new developments and promoting cultural tourism can also contribute to economic resilience.

Smart City Technologies and Innovations in Chinese Urban Development:

Smart city technologies offer innovative solutions to enhance urban resilience. By integrating sensors, data analytics, and automation systems, Chinese cities can improve disaster preparedness, response, and recovery. For example, real-time monitoring systems can detect early warning signs of natural disasters, enabling prompt evacuation and resource allocation.

Urban Transportation Systems and Infrastructure in New Chinese Cities:

Well-planned transportation systems and infrastructure are critical for disaster resilience. Chinese cities can enhance their transportation networks by incorporating multiple modes of transit, improving connectivity, and implementing intelligent traffic management systems. In the event of a disaster, efficient transportation systems can facilitate evacuation and emergency response.

Vertical Farming and Urban Agriculture in Chinese Urban Planning:

Vertical farming and urban agriculture contribute to both food security and disaster resilience. By utilizing vertical space and adopting innovative farming techniques, Chinese cities can reduce their reliance on external food sources. Additionally, urban agriculture can help mitigate the impacts of climate change by reducing carbon emissions and improving air quality.

Eco-friendly and Green Building Practices in New Chinese Cities:

Green building practices promote sustainability and resilience in Chinese cities. By incorporating energy-efficient designs, utilizing eco-friendly materials, and implementing green roofs and walls, buildings can withstand natural disasters more effectively. Additionally, green buildings contribute to reducing carbon emissions and improving indoor air quality.

Social and Community Development in Chinese Urban Areas:

Social development is crucial for building resilience in Chinese cities. By fostering inclusive communities, promoting social cohesion, and investing in education and healthcare, urban planners can enhance the resilience of vulnerable populations. Empowering communities to actively participate in disaster management and recovery efforts is also essential.

Urban Resilience and Disaster Management in New Chinese Cities:

Disaster management strategies should be an integral part of urban planning in Chinese cities. This includes developing early warning systems, establishing evacuation plans, and enhancing emergency response capabilities. Additionally, promoting community resilience through education and training programs can improve the overall preparedness of cities.

Urban Poverty Alleviation and Inclusive Growth Strategies in Chinese Cities:

Addressing urban poverty is crucial for building resilience against disasters. By implementing inclusive growth strategies, providing affordable housing, and creating employment opportunities, Chinese cities can reduce vulnerability and enhance resilience. Social safety nets and targeted poverty alleviation programs should also be prioritized.

Urban Design and Architectural Trends in New Chinese Cities:

Urban design and architectural trends should align with the principles of resilience in Chinese cities. This includes designing flexible spaces that can adapt to changing needs, utilizing sustainable materials, and integrating nature into the built environment. By embracing innovative design concepts, Chinese cities can enhance their resilience and create sustainable urban environments.

Conclusion:

Building resilience against natural and man-made disasters is a multifaceted challenge for urban planners in Chinese cities. By incorporating sustainable urban planning, cultural preservation, smart city technologies, transportation systems, vertical farming, eco-friendly building practices, social development, disaster management, poverty alleviation, and urban design trends, Chinese cities can become more resilient, ensuring the well-being and safety of their residents.

Chapter 10: Urban Poverty Alleviation and Inclusive Growth Strategies in Chinese Cities

Challenges and dimensions of urban poverty in Chinese cities

In recent years, Chinese cities have experienced rapid urbanization and economic growth. However, alongside this development, there has been a rise in urban poverty, posing significant challenges to sustainable urban planning and inclusive growth strategies. This subchapter will explore the various dimensions of urban poverty in Chinese cities, shedding light on the social and economic disparities that exist within these urban areas.

One of the key challenges in addressing urban poverty in Chinese cities is the widening wealth gap. As the country's economy continues to grow, the rich-poor divide has become more pronounced, with a significant portion of the population struggling to meet their basic needs. This inequality is further exacerbated by the high cost of living in urban areas, making it difficult for low-income residents to afford housing, healthcare, and education.

Another dimension of urban poverty in Chinese cities is the issue of migrant workers. Millions of rural residents migrate to cities in search of better job opportunities, but often find themselves trapped in low-paying and unstable employment. These migrant workers face numerous challenges, including inadequate access to social services, limited job security, and discrimination.

Furthermore, urban poverty in Chinese cities is also closely intertwined with issues of social exclusion and limited access to public services. Many low-income residents are concentrated in marginalized neighborhoods with inadequate infrastructure, limited transportation options, and poor access to quality education and healthcare. These factors perpetuate cycles of poverty and hinder social mobility for disadvantaged communities.

To address these challenges, sustainable urban planning in Chinese cities needs to prioritize inclusive growth strategies and social welfare programs. Efforts should be made to develop affordable housing options, improve access to public services, and enhance job opportunities for low-income residents. Additionally, cultural preservation and heritage conservation should be integrated into urban planning to ensure that urban development does not erode the social fabric of communities.

Furthermore, the adoption of smart city technologies and innovations can play a significant role in alleviating urban poverty. By leveraging data and technology, urban planners can develop efficient transportation systems, optimize resource allocation, and improve service delivery to underserved communities.

In conclusion, urban poverty in Chinese cities presents multifaceted challenges that require a holistic approach from urban planners. By addressing the dimensions of urban poverty, such as the wealth gap, migrant workers' plight, social exclusion, and limited access to public services, sustainable and inclusive urban development can be achieved. By integrating cultural preservation, smart city technologies, and social welfare programs into urban planning, Chinese cities can strive towards a future where no citizen is left behind.

Policies and programs for poverty alleviation in urban areas

The rapid urbanization of Chinese cities has brought about economic growth and development, but it has also led to an increase in urban poverty. As urban planners, it is crucial to address this issue and implement effective policies and programs for poverty alleviation in urban areas. This subchapter will explore various strategies and initiatives aimed at reducing poverty and promoting inclusive growth in Chinese cities.

One key policy is the creation of affordable housing programs. The Chinese government has recognized the need for affordable housing and has implemented programs such as the Affordable Housing Project. This initiative aims to provide low-income individuals and families with access to affordable housing options, reducing the burden of housing costs and improving their quality of life.

Another important policy is the promotion of inclusive economic development. By encouraging the growth of industries that provide job opportunities for low-income individuals, urban planners can create an inclusive economy that benefits all segments of society. This can be achieved through the establishment of economic zones and industrial parks that prioritize the creation of jobs for the urban poor.

In addition to these policies, there are several programs focused on skills development and education. These initiatives aim to equip individuals with the necessary skills and knowledge to secure better employment opportunities. Vocational training programs and scholarships for low-income students are examples of such programs that can empower individuals and lift them out of poverty.

Furthermore, social welfare programs play a crucial role in poverty alleviation. By providing access to healthcare, social security, and other basic services, these programs ensure that individuals have a safety net to fall back on in times of need. Urban planners can work closely with social welfare agencies to ensure that these services are accessible and efficient in reaching the urban poor.

Lastly, community development and empowerment initiatives are essential for poverty alleviation. By promoting community participation and engagement, urban planners can empower individuals and communities to take charge of their own development. This can be done through the establishment of community centers, urban gardens, and other spaces that foster social cohesion and encourage community involvement.

In conclusion, poverty alleviation in urban areas requires a multi-faceted approach that combines affordable housing, inclusive economic development, education, social welfare programs, and community empowerment. As urban planners, it is our responsibility to design and implement policies and programs that address the unique challenges faced by the urban poor in Chinese cities. By doing so, we can create sustainable, inclusive, and prosperous cities for all.

Promoting inclusive growth and reducing urban inequality in China

China's unprecedented urbanization has brought about rapid economic growth and development, but it has also led to significant challenges, such as increasing urban inequality and social disparities. In order to address these issues and promote inclusive growth, urban planners in China need to adopt a holistic approach that integrates social, economic, and environmental considerations into their planning and design processes.

One key aspect of promoting inclusive growth is sustainable urban planning. Chinese cities have been grappling with issues such as air pollution, water scarcity, and waste management, which have a direct impact on the quality of life and well-being of their residents. By incorporating sustainable practices, such as green building practices, vertical farming, and eco-friendly infrastructure, urban planners can create healthier and more livable cities for all residents, regardless of their socio-economic background.

Cultural preservation and heritage conservation also play a crucial role in promoting inclusive growth. Many new Chinese cities have been built on the foundations of historic towns and villages, which are rich in cultural heritage. By preserving and integrating these historic elements into the urban fabric, urban planners can create a sense of place and identity, while also promoting tourism and economic development.

Smart city technologies and innovations offer another avenue for promoting inclusive growth. By leveraging technology and data, urban planners can improve the efficiency and effectiveness of urban services, such as transportation, energy, and public safety. This can help bridge the digital divide and ensure that all residents have access to essential services and opportunities.

Urban transportation systems and infrastructure also play a critical role in promoting inclusive growth. By investing in public transportation, pedestrian-friendly infrastructure, and non-motorized transport options, urban planners can ensure that all residents have access to affordable and efficient transportation, regardless of their income or location.

In addition to physical infrastructure, social and community development are also important for promoting inclusive growth. By creating vibrant and inclusive public spaces, promoting community participation, and providing social services, urban planners can foster social cohesion and improve the overall well-being of residents.

Furthermore, urban resilience and disaster management are essential for ensuring the sustainable and inclusive development of Chinese cities. By integrating resilience strategies into urban planning, such as climate change adaptation measures and disaster risk reduction, urban planners can protect vulnerable communities and ensure their long-term sustainability.

Lastly, inclusive growth strategies should prioritize poverty alleviation and address the needs of marginalized communities. By investing in education, healthcare, and social welfare programs, urban planners can empower disadvantaged groups and reduce urban poverty.

In conclusion, promoting inclusive growth and reducing urban inequality in China requires a comprehensive and integrated approach that considers social, economic, and environmental factors. By adopting sustainable practices, preserving cultural heritage, leveraging smart city technologies, improving transportation systems, promoting social and community development, enhancing urban resilience, and prioritizing poverty alleviation, urban planners can create more equitable and livable cities for all residents.

Chapter 11: Urban Design and Architectural Trends in New Chinese Cities

Contemporary architectural trends in Chinese urban development

China's rapid urbanization has brought about numerous architectural trends that reflect the country's unique cultural heritage, as well as its aspirations for sustainable and innovative urban development. This subchapter explores the key trends shaping the architectural landscape of new Chinese cities and their implications for urban planners.

Sustainable urban planning in Chinese cities has become a top priority in recent years. With the aim of reducing carbon emissions and promoting energy efficiency, Chinese cities are embracing eco-friendly building practices and incorporating green spaces into their urban fabric. From vertical farming and urban agriculture initiatives to the integration of renewable energy sources, sustainable urban planning in China is leading the way in creating environmentally conscious cities.

Cultural preservation and heritage conservation in new Chinese cities are also gaining prominence. As urbanization continues at a rapid pace, there is a growing recognition of the importance of preserving and revitalizing China's rich cultural heritage. In response, urban planners are adopting innovative strategies to protect historical sites and integrate them into contemporary urban designs, creating a harmonious blend of old and new.

Smart city technologies and innovations are transforming Chinese urban development. With the advancement of digital technologies, Chinese cities are becoming increasingly connected and efficient. From smart transportation systems to the use of big data for urban planning, these innovations are improving the quality of life for residents and enhancing urban sustainability.

Urban transportation systems and infrastructure are being revolutionized in new Chinese cities. As urban populations grow, the need for efficient and sustainable transportation systems becomes paramount. Chinese cities are investing heavily in high-speed rail networks, metro systems, and bike-sharing programs to create seamless and eco-friendly transportation options for residents.

Vertical farming and urban agriculture are emerging as viable solutions to food security and sustainability challenges in Chinese urban planning. With limited arable land, vertical farming techniques are being employed to maximize space and increase crop yields. Urban agriculture initiatives are also promoting community engagement and healthy eating habits.

Eco-friendly and green building practices are becoming standard in new Chinese cities. From energy-efficient building designs to the use of sustainable materials, Chinese architects are prioritizing environmentally friendly construction methods. This not only reduces the carbon footprint of buildings but also creates healthier and more comfortable living environments for residents.

Social and community development is a key aspect of Chinese urban planning. Chinese cities are striving to create inclusive and livable communities that foster social interaction and well-being. From the design of public spaces to the provision of social amenities, urban planners are working towards creating vibrant and cohesive neighborhoods that cater to the needs of diverse populations.

Urban resilience and disaster management strategies are crucial for Chinese cities, given their vulnerability to natural disasters. Chinese urban planners are adopting innovative approaches to enhance the resilience of cities, including the use of green infrastructure, flood-resistant designs, and early warning systems.

Urban poverty alleviation and inclusive growth strategies are of paramount importance in Chinese cities. As income disparities persist, urban planners are implementing policies and programs to address poverty and promote inclusive growth. These initiatives focus on providing affordable housing, improving access to education and healthcare, and creating employment opportunities for marginalized communities.

Finally, urban design and architectural trends in new Chinese cities are characterized by a blend of traditional and contemporary influences. Chinese architects are reinterpreting traditional architectural elements and incorporating them into modern designs, creating a unique architectural language that reflects China's rich cultural heritage.

Overall, the contemporary architectural trends in Chinese urban development reflect a commitment to sustainability, cultural preservation, innovation, and social well-being. By understanding and incorporating these trends into their planning strategies, urban planners can contribute to the creation of livable, resilient, and inclusive cities in China.

Integration of traditional and modern architectural elements in new Chinese cities

In recent years, China has experienced rapid urbanization, resulting in the creation of new cities across the country. As urban planners, it is essential to consider the integration of traditional and modern architectural elements in these new Chinese cities. This subchapter will explore the significance of incorporating traditional architectural elements into the design of modern cities, and how this integration can contribute to sustainable urban planning, cultural preservation, smart city technologies, transportation systems, vertical farming, eco-friendly building practices, social and community development, urban resilience, poverty alleviation, and urban design trends.

Sustainable urban planning in Chinese cities requires careful consideration of the environmental, social, and economic impacts of new developments. By integrating traditional architectural elements, such as courtyard houses and wooden structures, into the design of new buildings, planners can contribute to the preservation of cultural heritage while providing sustainable solutions for the future.

Cultural preservation and heritage conservation in new Chinese cities play a crucial role in maintaining the country's rich history and traditions. By incorporating traditional architectural elements, such as roof designs and decorative motifs, into modern buildings, planners can create a harmonious blend of the old and the new, preserving cultural identity while promoting cultural exchange.

Smart city technologies and innovations in Chinese urban development can benefit from the integration of traditional architectural elements. By utilizing traditional building materials and techniques, such as bamboo and natural ventilation systems, planners can create more energy-efficient and sustainable cities, reducing the reliance on artificial technologies.

Urban transportation systems and infrastructure in new Chinese cities can also benefit from the integration of traditional architectural elements. By incorporating pedestrian-friendly streetscapes, traditional archways, and public spaces inspired by traditional Chinese gardens, planners can create a more walkable and enjoyable urban environment.

Vertical farming and urban agriculture in Chinese urban planning can be enhanced by integrating traditional agricultural practices into the design of new cities. By incorporating rooftop gardens, community farms, and green spaces inspired by traditional Chinese agricultural techniques, planners can promote sustainable food production and enhance the quality of life for urban residents.

Eco-friendly and green building practices in new Chinese cities can be achieved by integrating traditional architectural elements. By utilizing sustainable materials, such as reclaimed wood and bamboo, and incorporating natural ventilation systems and green roofs, planners can reduce the environmental impact of new developments and create healthier living environments.

Social and community development in Chinese urban areas can be fostered by integrating traditional architectural elements that promote a sense of community and cultural identity. By designing public spaces that incorporate traditional Chinese pavilions, courtyards, and communal gathering areas, planners can create spaces that encourage social interaction and community engagement.

Urban resilience and disaster management in new Chinese cities can benefit from the integration of traditional architectural elements that have proven to withstand natural disasters. By incorporating earthquake-resistant techniques and materials inspired by traditional Chinese architecture, planners can create more resilient cities that can withstand the challenges of the future.

Urban poverty alleviation and inclusive growth strategies in Chinese cities can be supported by integrating traditional architectural elements that promote affordable housing and economic opportunities. By incorporating traditional courtyard housing designs and mixed-use developments, planners can create inclusive communities that provide affordable housing options and support local businesses.

Urban design and architectural trends in new Chinese cities can be enriched by the integration of traditional elements. By incorporating traditional motifs, materials, and styles into the design of new buildings, planners can create unique and visually appealing cityscapes that reflect the rich cultural heritage of China while embracing modern design principles.

In conclusion, the integration of traditional and modern architectural elements in new Chinese cities is of utmost importance for urban planners. By considering and incorporating traditional architectural elements, planners can contribute to sustainable urban planning, cultural preservation, smart city technologies, transportation systems, vertical farming, eco-friendly building practices, social and community development, urban resilience, poverty alleviation, and urban design trends in Chinese cities.

Future directions and possibilities in urban design in China

As urban planners, it is crucial for us to stay ahead of the curve and anticipate the future directions and possibilities in urban design in China. With the rapid pace of urbanization and the unique challenges faced by Chinese cities, it is important to explore innovative solutions that promote sustainable urban planning, cultural preservation, smart city technologies, efficient transportation systems, vertical farming, eco-friendly building practices, social development, urban resilience, poverty alleviation, and inclusive growth strategies. This subchapter will delve into these topics, showcasing the potential future trends and directions in urban design in China.

Sustainable urban planning in Chinese cities is of utmost importance to ensure a balance between economic growth and environmental protection. Integrating green spaces, promoting energy-efficient buildings, and implementing sustainable transportation systems are some of the key aspects that will shape the future of urban design in China.

Cultural preservation and heritage conservation in new Chinese cities should be given due attention to maintain the rich cultural heritage of the country. Combining modern architectural trends with traditional elements can create a unique identity for new Chinese cities while preserving their historical significance.

Smart city technologies and innovations in Chinese urban development have the potential to revolutionize urban design. From advanced transportation systems to efficient energy management, incorporating smart technologies can enhance the quality of life for residents and improve the overall efficiency of cities.

Urban transportation systems and infrastructure in new Chinese cities need to be designed with a focus on reducing congestion, improving accessibility, and promoting sustainable modes of transport. Embracing electric vehicles, developing efficient public transportation networks, and implementing smart traffic management systems will be essential in shaping the future of urban transportation in China.

Vertical farming and urban agriculture in Chinese urban planning can address the challenges of food security and promote sustainable living. Integrating vertical farms into urban design can provide fresh produce, reduce the carbon footprint of food production, and create green spaces within cities.

Eco-friendly and green building practices in new Chinese cities should be encouraged to minimize the environmental impact of construction. Incorporating renewable energy sources, using sustainable materials, and implementing energy-efficient designs can lead to greener and more sustainable urban environments.

Social and community development in Chinese urban areas is crucial for fostering a sense of belonging and improving the quality of life for residents. Creating inclusive spaces, promoting social integration, and investing in community infrastructure can contribute to the overall well-being of urban populations.

Urban resilience and disaster management in new Chinese cities need to be prioritized to mitigate the risks associated with natural disasters and climate change. Developing resilient infrastructure, implementing early warning systems, and integrating disaster management strategies into urban design can enhance the ability of cities to withstand and recover from adverse events.

Urban poverty alleviation and inclusive growth strategies in Chinese cities should be integral to urban design. Creating affordable housing, improving access to education and healthcare, and promoting economic opportunities can help uplift marginalized communities and foster inclusive growth.

In conclusion, the future of urban design in China lies in embracing sustainable practices, preserving cultural heritage, adopting smart technologies, improving transportation systems, integrating vertical farming, promoting eco-friendly building practices, facilitating social development, enhancing urban resilience, implementing poverty alleviation strategies, and staying abreast of architectural trends. By addressing these key areas, urban planners can shape the future of Chinese cities, creating livable, resilient, and inclusive urban environments for generations to come.

Chapter 12: Conclusion

Summary of key findings

In the book "Designing the Future: Architectural Trends in New Chinese Cities," a comprehensive analysis of various aspects of urban development in China is presented. This summary highlights the key findings of the book that are relevant to urban planners and the specific niches of sustainable urban planning, cultural preservation, smart city technologies, urban transportation, vertical farming, eco-friendly building practices, social development, urban resilience, poverty alleviation, and urban design.

The findings indicate that sustainable urban planning in Chinese cities is gaining momentum. City planners are focusing on creating environmentally-friendly and resource-efficient urban areas. They are incorporating green spaces, promoting renewable energy sources, and implementing measures to reduce pollution and waste.

Cultural preservation and heritage conservation have become crucial in new Chinese cities. The book highlights the importance of preserving historical and cultural sites while accommodating modern infrastructure. It explores the challenges of striking a balance between development and cultural preservation.

Smart city technologies and innovations are rapidly transforming Chinese urban development. The book showcases the integration of advanced technologies such as artificial intelligence, Internet of Things, and big data analytics in improving urban services, enhancing efficiency, and creating a better quality of life for residents.

Urban transportation systems and infrastructure in Chinese cities are undergoing significant advancements. The book examines the expansion of public transportation networks, the introduction of electric vehicles, and the implementation of smart traffic management systems to address the challenges of congestion and pollution.

Vertical farming and urban agriculture are emerging as key strategies in Chinese urban planning. The book discusses the benefits of vertical farming in maximizing land use, reducing transportation costs, and promoting food security in densely populated urban areas.

Eco-friendly and green building practices are gaining popularity in new Chinese cities. The book highlights the use of sustainable materials, energy-efficient designs, and green roofs in creating environmentally-friendly buildings that contribute to a healthier and more sustainable urban environment.

Social and community development is a critical aspect of Chinese urban areas. The book explores the importance of creating inclusive and vibrant communities that foster social cohesion, promote cultural diversity, and provide adequate social amenities for residents.

Urban resilience and disaster management strategies are being implemented in new Chinese cities. The book examines how cities are preparing for and mitigating the impact of natural disasters, climate change, and other vulnerabilities through improved infrastructure, early warning systems, and community engagement.

Urban poverty alleviation and inclusive growth strategies are crucial for achieving sustainable development in Chinese cities. The book explores various initiatives aimed at reducing poverty, improving access to basic services, and promoting inclusive economic growth in urban areas.

Lastly, the book delves into the latest urban design and architectural trends in new Chinese cities. It showcases innovative designs that blend modern aesthetics with cultural elements, creating unique urban landscapes that reflect China's rich heritage and aspirations for the future.

Overall, "Designing the Future: Architectural Trends in New Chinese Cities" provides valuable insights for urban planners and professionals in various niches of urban development in China. The book emphasizes the importance of sustainable practices, cultural preservation, technological advancements, and social development in shaping the cities of the future.

Implications for the future of Chinese urban planning

As urban planners, it is crucial to understand the implications of current trends in Chinese urban planning and how they will shape the future of cities in China. In this subchapter, we will explore several key areas that will have a significant impact on the future of Chinese urban planning.

One of the primary concerns in Chinese urban planning is sustainability. With the rapid urbanization occurring in the country, it is essential to develop sustainable urban planning strategies that minimize environmental impact and promote long-term resilience. This includes incorporating renewable energy sources, implementing green building practices, and focusing on eco-friendly transportation systems. By prioritizing sustainable urban planning, Chinese cities can become models for sustainable development worldwide.

Cultural preservation and heritage conservation also play a vital role in the future of Chinese urban planning. As cities expand and modernize, it is crucial to preserve and protect their unique cultural heritage. This can be achieved through adaptive reuse of historic buildings, promoting cultural tourism, and integrating traditional architectural elements into new developments. By preserving their cultural identity, Chinese cities can maintain a sense of place and attract visitors from around the world.

Smart city technologies and innovations are transforming Chinese urban development. From smart grids to intelligent transportation systems, incorporating technology into urban planning is essential for creating efficient and livable cities. Chinese cities are embracing smart city initiatives, such as the use of big data for urban management and the integration of Internet of Things (IoT) devices for real-time monitoring. These technologies will revolutionize the way cities are planned and managed in the future.

Urban transportation systems and infrastructure are critical for the future of Chinese cities. With the increase in population and economic activity, the demand for efficient transportation systems is growing. Chinese urban planners are investing in the development of public transportation networks, including high-speed rail, subway systems, and bus rapid transit. By prioritizing public transportation and reducing reliance on private vehicles, Chinese cities can alleviate traffic congestion and reduce air pollution.

Vertical farming and urban agriculture are emerging trends in Chinese urban planning. As urban areas expand, there is a growing need to produce food locally and sustainably. Vertical farming techniques, such as hydroponics and aeroponics, allow for the cultivation of crops within urban environments. By integrating agriculture into urban planning, Chinese cities can become more self-sufficient in food production and improve food security.

Eco-friendly and green building practices are becoming increasingly important in Chinese urban planning. Green building certifications, such as LEED and BREEAM, are being adopted to ensure that new developments meet environmental sustainability standards. By promoting energy-efficient building designs, renewable energy integration, and sustainable materials, Chinese cities can reduce their carbon footprint and create healthier living environments for residents.

Social and community development are crucial aspects of Chinese urban planning. As cities grow, it is important to foster social cohesion and create inclusive communities. This includes providing affordable housing options, developing public spaces for recreation and social interaction, and promoting community engagement in decision-making processes. By prioritizing social and community development, Chinese cities can enhance the quality of life for their residents and create more equitable urban environments.

Urban resilience and disaster management are critical considerations in Chinese urban planning. With the increasing frequency and intensity of natural disasters, it is essential to design cities that can withstand and recover from these events. This includes implementing resilient infrastructure, developing emergency response plans, and integrating green infrastructure to mitigate the impact of climate change. By prioritizing urban resilience, Chinese cities can reduce the vulnerability of their residents and enhance their ability to bounce back from disasters.

Urban poverty alleviation and inclusive growth strategies are key challenges in Chinese cities. As urbanization continues, it is important to address income inequality and ensure that the benefits of urban development are shared by all residents. This includes implementing inclusive economic policies, providing affordable housing options, and investing in education and job training programs. By adopting inclusive growth strategies, Chinese cities can create more equitable and sustainable urban environments.

Finally, urban design and architectural trends are constantly evolving in Chinese cities. From futuristic skyline designs to the integration of traditional architectural elements, Chinese cities are at the forefront of innovative urban design. By embracing architectural trends that prioritize sustainability, cultural preservation, and livability, Chinese cities can create unique and vibrant urban environments that inspire residents and visitors alike.

In conclusion, the future of Chinese urban planning will be shaped by sustainable development practices, cultural preservation, smart city technologies, efficient transportation systems, vertical farming, eco-friendly building practices, social and community development, urban resilience, poverty alleviation strategies, and innovative urban design trends. As urban planners, it is essential to stay abreast of these implications and incorporate them into our planning strategies to create cities that are livable, resilient, and sustainable for future generations.

Call to action for urban planners in shaping the future of Chinese cities.

Call to Action for Urban Planners in Shaping the Future of Chinese Cities

As urban planners, you hold a crucial role in shaping the future of Chinese cities. With rapid urbanization and the challenges that come along with it, it is imperative that we focus on sustainable, inclusive, and innovative approaches to urban planning. In this subchapter, we will explore the various aspects of urban development in China and call upon you to take action in creating cities that are not only aesthetically pleasing but also socially, economically, and environmentally sustainable.

Sustainable urban planning in Chinese cities is of utmost importance. As the population continues to grow, it is crucial to develop cities that are resource-efficient, reduce carbon emissions, and promote a healthy living environment. Integrating green spaces, renewable energy sources, and efficient waste management systems are some of the key strategies that can be implemented to achieve sustainable urban development.

Preserving cultural heritage in new Chinese cities is another essential aspect that should not be overlooked. While modernization is necessary, it is equally important to protect and honor the rich cultural heritage of China. By incorporating traditional architectural elements and preserving historical sites, we can create cities that are a harmonious blend of the past and the future.

Smart city technologies and innovations play a pivotal role in Chinese urban development. Embracing digital advancements can lead to improved efficiency, enhanced connectivity, and better quality of life for residents. From smart transportation systems to energy-efficient buildings, the integration of technology will revolutionize urban planning in China.

Urban transportation systems and infrastructure are key to ensuring smooth mobility and reducing congestion in new Chinese cities. By investing in sustainable modes of transportation such as mass transit systems, bike-sharing programs, and pedestrian-friendly infrastructure, we can create cities that are less reliant on private cars and promote a healthier, more accessible urban environment.

Vertical farming and urban agriculture present innovative solutions to food security and sustainable living in Chinese cities. By utilizing vertical space and integrating agriculture into urban areas, we can reduce the carbon footprint associated with food production and enhance the availability of fresh, locally grown produce.

Eco-friendly and green building practices should be at the forefront of urban planning in China. By utilizing sustainable materials, implementing energy-efficient designs, and incorporating green spaces into our cities, we can create buildings that minimize environmental impact and promote a healthier, more sustainable lifestyle for residents.

Social and community development are vital aspects of urban planning. Creating spaces that foster social interaction, promote inclusivity, and address the needs of diverse communities is essential for building cohesive and resilient cities.

In the face of increasing natural disasters and climate change, urban resilience and disaster management must be integrated into the planning process. By considering the potential risks and implementing measures to mitigate them, we can create cities that are better prepared to withstand and recover from disasters.

Addressing urban poverty and promoting inclusive growth strategies are critical for creating cities that provide equal opportunities for all residents. By implementing policies that promote affordable housing, job creation, and access to basic services, we can work towards reducing inequality and improving the quality of life for all.

Lastly, urban design and architectural trends should reflect the values and aspirations of the people. By incorporating cultural influences, embracing innovative designs, and prioritizing sustainability, we can create cities that are not only functional but also visually appealing and reflective of the unique Chinese identity.

As urban planners, the responsibility lies upon us to shape the future of Chinese cities. By taking action in these various areas, we can create cities that are sustainable, inclusive, and resilient. Let us work together to design a future that we can be proud of, a future that reflects the values and aspirations of the Chinese people.

www.ingramcontent.com/pod-product-compliance
Lightning Source LLC
Chambersburg PA
CBHW031449130726
47989CB00003B/1319